STEP-BY-STEP
Wedding Flowers

STEP-BY-STEP
Wedding Flowers

A PRACTICAL AND INSPIRATIONAL GUIDE TO CREATING BEAUTIFUL
AND MEMORABLE FLOWERS FOR YOUR WEDDING

Kally Ellis and Ercole Moroni

Photography by James Duncan

ACROPOLIS BOOKS

First published in 1994 by Lorenz Books

© Anness Publishing Limited

Lorenz Books is an imprint of
Anness Publishing Limited
Boundary Row Studios
1 Boundary Row
London SE1 8HP

A CIP catalogue record for this book
is available from the British Library

ISBN 1 85967 003 2

Distributed in Australia by Treasure Press

Editorial Director: Joanna Lorenz
Series Editor: Lindsay Porter
Designers: Peter Butler, Derek Copsey
Photographer: James Duncan
Stylists: Gloria Nicol, Kally Ellis, Ercole Moroni

Printed and bound in Italy by Graphicom S.r.l., Vicenza

CONTENTS

INTRODUCTION

*F*lowers communicate in a way that words never can. They sum up feelings, evoke moods and express emotions. A wedding is a time for celebration, a time for making vows and choices. Flowers don't last forever, but the memory of your wedding blooms certainly will, so it's worth taking time to consider all the options available to you. It's not simply a question of choosing the right colours to match your dress. Everything about you on your wedding day will create an impression, a reflection of yourself, and the floral displays you select are an intrinsic part of the celebrations. The aim of this book is not only to help you make that selection, but to show you how to achieve the flowers you always dreamed of on your wedding day.

Just as styles move in and out of fashion, the world of flowers is constantly evolving. Today, anything goes; although bouquets vary in size and shape, current trends are moving away from the wired shower bouquet towards the lighter, more free style of floristry. The look is less rigid and more natural, but still demands great control and skill. The abundance of different flowers available nowadays means that there are no hard and fast rules any more. This book is dedicated to all those brides who know there is more to their wedding bouquet than just carnations, roses and a few desultory ferns. Remember, the only limit to what you can achieve is your own imagination. Be brave; we feel sure you'll agree that it's worth taking a few risks.

Flower Care

You will probably be planning your wedding well in advance, so remember to take into account seasonal availability. Flowers are at their cheapest when they are in season. It is useful to know, however, that nowadays most flowers are available most of the year.

These are, of course, force-grown and on the whole less robust and much more expensive. You will need to buy your flowers at least two or three days prior to the wedding day so that the blooms are open and at their most beautiful.

CONDITIONING FLOWERS

Once you have chosen your flowers, the way in which you handle them will make a huge difference to their lasting qualities. The quicker they are cut and put in water, the better. Similarly, make sure that when you are working with your flowers they are kept constantly refreshed and cool, preferably in a dark place.

You'll need a selection of buckets to give your blooms a good long drink, too. Always make sure buckets are kept clean as bacteria will breed remarkably quickly, especially in warmer weather. The growth of bacteria is likely to have an adverse effect upon your flowers and could prevent blooms from opening properly, or shorten their life span.

Conditioning your flowers is very important. For the most part all you will need to do is remove damaged foliage, particularly the foliage below the waterline. Always make a slanting cut at the base of the stem. Woody stems do not take up moisture as quickly as soft stems and therefore should have a longer period in deep water before being used.

Some flower varieties will need special care and attention:

Hard, woody stems (eg lilac) The base of the stem should be hammered to split the wood fibres, and the bark removed 2.5 cm (1 in) from the bottom. Dunk the stem ends in boiling water for 30 seconds then plunge the flowers up to their necks in warm water for a few hours. Any limp flowers will be revitalized.

Stems which bleed (eg euphorbia) Once the stem is cut, seal by placing the cut surface over a naked flame for a few seconds. Alternatively dip the cut ends in a shallow tray of boiling water for up to 30 seconds.

Hollow stems (eg amaryllis, delphinium) Invert the flowers and fill the hollow stem with water. Plug the end with cotton wool and stand them immediately in a deep bucket of water. In the case of amaryllis secure an elastic band around the base of the stalk. This prevents the tissue from splitting and curling at the base.

Roses Cut at an angle and split at the base. Carefully remove all thorns and the base leaves. Tightly wrap the heads together in a roll of stiff paper and stand in deep water. Any roses which are limp should be given the hot water treatment.

Foliage Care

In recent times, there has been a complete revolution in greenery. Once, foliage was added sparingly to bouquets and other floral arrangements and the varieties used were limited and unadventurous. Now, greenery is more liberally used and is recognized by most serious florists as being every bit as important as the flowers themselves. With increasing frequency, foliage has been used to form the entire composition, and the wealth of textures and colours the different varieties provide rival the most stunning flowers.

There really is no limit to the sort of foliage which is available now; if you have trouble finding greenery at your local florist, don't despair – hunt it down yourself! There is an abundance of material all around us.

CONDITIONING FOLIAGE
As with the flowers, foliage should be handled with great care using only clean water from the tap and clean buckets. These should be changed frequently to minimize bacterial growth and odours.

Nearly all foliage stems are woody so the conditioning of them is fairly straightforward. You will need a pair of secateurs (pruning shears) for the extra thick branches and a wooden mallet or hammer to bash the ends of the stems. This process splits the stems and helps with water absorption. All leaves below the waterline should be removed. Allow to have a drink for a few hours before needed. Limp foliage will pick up better if the stems are immersed in warm water.

Opposite: *Give flowers a good long soak in water before arranging to ensure they are in top condition.*

Right: *Foliage need not take second place to flowers. There are enough interesting varieties to use them as a focal point.*

What You'll Need

To achieve perfect results, you will need the tools of the trade. Your local sundries supplier (you'll find these at the nearest flower market) will have everything you require from wires to glue guns and colour sprays.

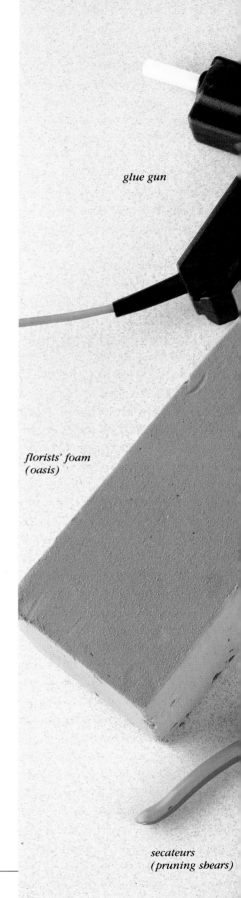

glue gun

florists' foam (oasis)

secateurs (pruning shears)

Florists' foam (oasis)
Two types are available: the green variety is used to support the stems of fresh flowers, keeping them fresh and moist. The brown variety is used for dried-flower arrangements and holding wired stems in place.

Florists' foam tape
Choose from two thicknesses available; it is used to secure florists' foam into baskets or plastic trays.

Florists' knife
Essential for cleaning stems and cutting wet florists' foam (oasis).

Florists' scissors
An essential aid, these are used for all manner of tasks from trimming flowers and foliage to cutting ribbon. They also have a special notch for cutting wires.

Gardening twine
This is used for tying posies and bouquets and can be bought in reels.

Gutta percha (floral) tape
Used for covering wire stems, the natural green colour makes excellent camouflage and is most commonly used.

Glue gun
Used mainly in dried work, but can also be used to glue fresh moss to chicken wire.

Pins
Ideal for holding ribbon in place when covering a handle and for securing buttonholes and corsages to lapels.

Rose stripper
This tool removes the thorns and leaves from rose stems.

Secateurs (pruning shears)
Useful for extra thick stems.

Wires
Wire is needed for making corsages, head-dresses, buttonholes, etc. Silver wire and stub (floral) wire are available in varying degrees of thickness.

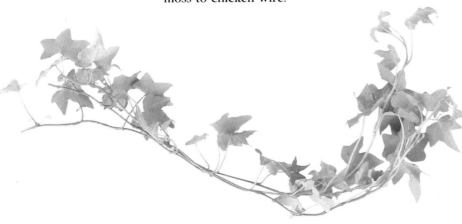

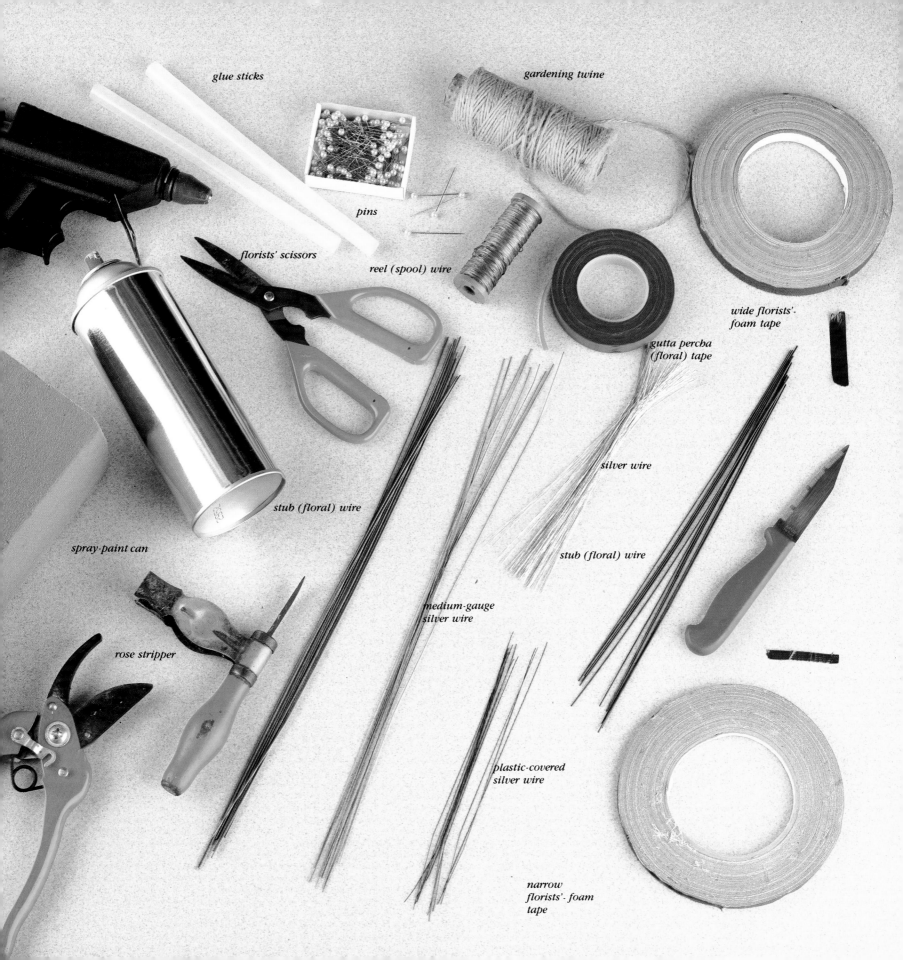

glue sticks

gardening twine

pins

florists' scissors

reel (spool) wire

wide florists'-
foam tape

gutta percha
(floral) tape

silver wire

stub (floral) wire

spray-paint can

stub (floral) wire

rose stripper

medium-gauge
silver wire

plastic-covered
silver wire

narrow
florists'- foam
tape

TECHNIQUES

The flowers and foliage used in wedding arrangements often need to be wired. It is common practice to remove the natural stems and replace them with wire, which is then covered in gutta percha (floral) tape. This not only reduces the weight of the finished product, but often gives a more delicate appearance.

Wiring should be neat, and as nearly invisible as possible. The general rule is to use the thinnest wire capable of supporting each flowerhead.

Wiring a Leaf

Leaves will have more flexibility and less weight when wired, essential for formal bouquets and head-dresses.

EQUIPMENT
scissors
silver wire
gutta percha (floral) tape

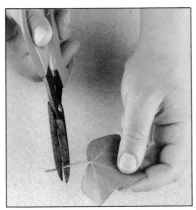

1 Cut the stem to about 2.5 cm (1 in) long.

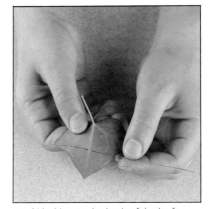

2 Working on the back of the leaf, thread a silver wire horizontally through the central vein, about two-thirds of the way up. Pull the wire through to a central position.

3 Draw both ends down, parallel to the natural stem.

4 Hold the leaf firmly between the thumb and forefinger and twist one wire around both the remaining stem and the other wire.

5 Attach the tape, just under the neck of the leaf.

6 Pulling the tape taut, twist the stem upwards until the wire is covered right down to the end.

7 Twist the tape onto itself to seal it, and break off the end.

Wiring a Rose

Use this technique with flowers such as roses and carnations, which have a solid calyx below the petals. If you decide to keep the sepals, pin these down with small hairpin-shaped pieces of silver wire to stop the bud opening. This is especially important to remember during hot weather.

EQUIPMENT
scissors
silver and stub (floral) wire
gutta percha (floral) tape

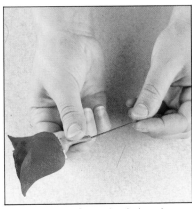

1 Cut off the flower just below the calyx and push a stub (floral) wire upwards through the remaining stem.

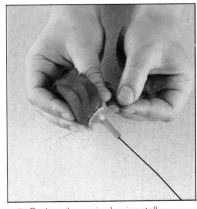

2 Push a silver wire horizontally through the calyx to a central position.

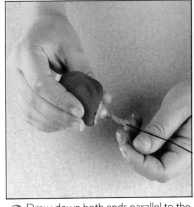

3 Draw down both ends parallel to the remaining stem, and twist one wire around the calyx and any other wires.

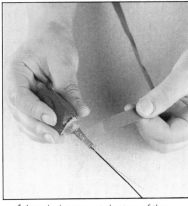

4 Attach the tape at the top of the calyx and twist the flower upwards. At the same time, stretch the tape tight as it winds around and down the false leg. Twist the tape onto itself to seal it, then break off the end.

The Single Leg Mount

This is probably the easiest method for wiring flowers which have a fairly sturdy natural stem.

EQUIPMENT
scissors
silver or stub (floral) wire
gutta percha (floral) tape

1 Cut the stem back to 5 cm (2 in). Place the wire across the neck of the bloom. Bend both ends parallel.

2 Twist one of the wire ends around the top of the stem, and the other wire all the way down to the bottom of the natural stem.

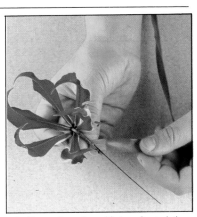

3 Cover the wire with tape by twisting the stem upwards while at the same time pulling the tape taut. Twist the tape onto itself to seal it and then cut the stem to the length required.

The Double Leg Mount

This method is the same whether you are wiring clusters of flowers, or a single head. It is used instead of the single leg mount for added support.

EQUIPMENT
scissors
silver or stub (floral) wire
gutta percha (floral) tape

1 Take a small bunch of lavender (or other flowers) and cut the stems to about 2.5 cm (1 in). Place an appropriate wire horizontally behind the stems, under the flowers, and bend the two ends of the wire downwards towards the stems.

2 Twist the longer wire end (a leg) firmly around the stems and around the other wire. Cut off the wires evenly and cover them with tape, finishing by twisting the tape onto itself to seal it, then breaking off the end.

Wiring Down

This method is used on flowerheads that have completely lost their natural stems or whose stems are so delicate that they need to be supported, for example delphinium heads that have been picked from the main flower.

EQUIPMENT
silver or stub (floral) wire
gutta percha (floral) tape

1 Rest the flowerhead between the thumb and the forefinger. Bend the wire in half to make a hairpin shape, with one leg longer than the other.

2 Push the two ends of the hairpin, longer leg first, down through the eye of the flower to form a small stitch.

3 Now twist the shorter leg around the longer leg and cover them with tape, finishing by twisting the tape onto itself to seal it, then breaking off the end.

Lengthening a False Stem

This method is used in shower bouquets, where very long stems are needed to form the outline shape.

EQUIPMENT
stub (floral) wire
gutta percha (floral) tape

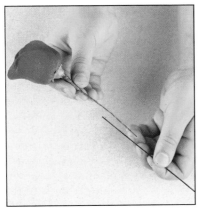

1 Take a stub (floral) wire and place it alongside the initial false leg, so that they overlap by about 5 cm (2 in).

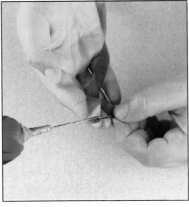

2 Attach the tape around both wires, and begin to bind them together.

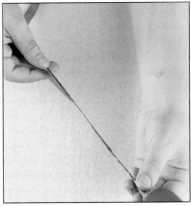

3 Twist the tape all the way down the new elongated false leg, stretching it as you go. Finish by twisting the tape onto itself to seal it, then breaking off the end.

Making a Bow

Use large, sumptuous bows to finish bouquets, to add interest to baskets and to trim swags.

1 Fold the ribbon to the required size, to form two loops in a figure-of-eight shape.

2 Hold the ribbon at the cross-over point, and repeat the figure-of-eight to give four loops.

3 Trim the remaining ribbon, and pinch the centre of the ribbon together.

4 Twist a separate length of ribbon firmly around the pinched ribbon and tie a knot at the back. Trim the ends, and pull the loops into shape.

COUNTRY WEDDING

veronica

*cow parsley
(Queen Anne's lace)*

W̶hat could be more inspiring than a country wedding in the height of summer? At no other time of the year can you find such a variety of colours, shapes and smells to create exciting and original floral designs. Fields are abundant with masses of wild flowers and foliage, so be daring in your selection.

scabious

delphinium

Groom's Buttonhole

A few selected blooms have been picked out and carefully arranged to create the groom's buttonhole. It is balanced by the positioning of the lavender at the top of the arrangement, and the draping white veronica at the base.

MATERIALS
scabious
ivy leaves
lavender
white veronica
white delphinium heads
pittosporum

EQUIPMENT
scissors
silver and stub (floral) wire
gutta percha (floral) tape
dressmakers' pin

1 Begin by wiring each flowerhead and leaf and covering the mechanics with tape. Place the main flower, the scabious, on top of the first and largest ivy leaf and tape them together.

2 Tape the lavender in the top left-hand corner and the white veronica in the bottom right-hand corner. Add the remaining material, and finish as for the Corsage.

Corsage

Designed for the mothers of the bride and groom, this corsage is large, but nevertheless, compactly arranged. Try to pick out the main colours, textures and flowerheads of the bride's bouquet.

MATERIALS
scabious
lavender
delphinium heads
cornflowers
nigella
cow parsley (Queen Anne's lace)
ivy leaves
snowberry

EQUIPMENT
scissors
silver and stub (floral) wire
gutta percha (floral) tape
dressmakers' pin

pittosporum

nigella

1 Wire all the flowers to be used with very fine wire in the double leg mount method (heavier flowers such as the scabious should be wired with slightly heavier silver wire). Flowers with delicate or thin stems, such as lavender, should be grouped together in threes and fives, and then wired. All the false legs should then be taped. The foliage should be stitched separately and then taped in the same manner. Take the first piece of foliage, an ivy leaf, and place it beneath the first sprig of lavender to create the point. Bind these together onto a mainstay wire with tape. Ensure that the mainstay wire is a few centimetres down the false legs, as this will help keep the spray supple.

2 Continue to position flowers, on alternate sides of the mainstay wire, so that the corsage gets wider and builds up higher. The closer you get to the centre, the larger the heads should be. Continue to frame the flowers with the stitched leaves, the largest leaves being placed behind the largest focal flowers. Do not place the flowers from the back of the corsage, or it will not lie flat.

3 The corsage has a return end that should be approximately half the length of the top of the spray. Tear off the tape at this point, and bend the wires to create a miniature handle. Place the last piece of ivy to create the corresponding point and bind onto the handle with the tape. Tear off the tape again, trim the ends of wire, taper them if necessary, and then wrap the stems once more with tape. A pin should be supplied so that the finished piece can be attached.

Bride's Bouquet

The graduated colours of the blue and white tones, together with the wildness of the hand-tied bouquet, give a free, light effect, while the loose style of the bouquet enhances the natural beauty of these flowers.

MATERIALS
snowberry
pittosporum
white and blue delphiniums
scabious
white veronica
lavender
cornflowers

nigella
cow parsley (Queen Anne's lace)
ribbon

EQUIPMENT
scissors
string or garden twine

3 Build up the basic shape with the rest of the foliage, to the size you wish to achieve. Now you are ready to begin to insert the flowers. Larger-headed flowers are arranged first. Always select flowers in odd numbers as this will produce a more balanced shape. Five stems of delphinium will be used here.

4 Slot them in around the edge of the foliage base and into the centre. If the spiral is properly constructed, a natural hole will emerge in the centre, allowing you to insert focal flowers more easily. Each delphinium should be equally spaced. The delphinium stem has a natural bend, which is ideal for this type of free-style bouquet.

1 Select the foliage to be used, and clean the base of the stems thoroughly. Take the first two stems of greenery, and cross one over the other to begin the spiral effect. Hold the stems loosely at the binding point. The looseness of your grip will determine the eventual size and shape of the bouquet; the looser your hold, the wider the posy.

2 Continue to build up the foliage base by angling the stems, always in the same direction across the binding point. At the same time, rotate the hand-tied bunch. Together, these two actions form the spiral shape.

5 Continue to add the flowers, angling the stems as you did with the foliage, and rotating the hand-tied bunch to achieve an even spread. Remember that the binding point should be two-thirds of the way down from the main arrangement, with the stems taking up the remaining third.

6 Start to introduce the filler flower heads, lavender, cornflower and nigella, arranging them in clusters for greater effect.

cornflower

pittosporum

ivy

7 The spiral shape is now well established and the remaining flower heads may be introduced with ease. The last flower to be used is the cow parsley (Queen Anne's lace), which is a particularly good filler, covering up any gaps that may have emerged. Note that the fillers have been slightly recessed for visual depth and body.

8 Tie the binding point with string or garden twine. Trim the stems evenly to the required length, and cover them with a suitable ribbon, tying the bow at the front of the bouquet.

Bride's Head-dress

Designed to be worn across the top of the head, this compact crescent of blooms echoes the cool tones of the bride's bouquet. Here the form is kept tight to provide greater control, the perfect foil to the wildness of the flowers. The width of the band is larger than usual to match the proportions of the bouquet.

MATERIALS
lavender
snowberry
delphinium heads
scabious
poppy heads
white veronica
cornflowers
nigella
cow parsley (Queen Anne's lace)
ivy leaves

EQUIPMENT
scissors
silver and stub (floral) wire
gutta percha (floral) tape

1 Select the flowers and foliage to be used and cut the stems at about 1.5 cm (½ in) from the heads of the flowers. Wire each flowerhead separately, using the single leg mount or the double leg mount method, depending on the delicacy of the flowerhead. All the leaves should be stitched carefully and wired. Tape all the wires.

2 Prepare the mainstay wire by binding together two heavy-gauge stub (floral) wires, staggering them to the appropriate length and then covering them with tape. Begin to mount the flowers and foliage, binding one flower onto the next with tape, and trimming the false legs as you go. Use the ivy leaves to frame the flowerheads.

3 The lavender stems should be wired together in groups for greater impact. Using the single leg mount method, wire three to five stems of lavender together then cover the stems with tape.

4 Build up the head-piece, gradually widening to the central peak. Curve the flowers and foliage over the side slightly, so that no gap is left between the head-dress and the hair. Group the white veronica on one side.

5 Work backwards using materials to balance the first side, tapering the second side to a point in exactly the same way. Break off the tape and press it down firmly with your fingertips. Adjust any flowers that may have moved.

Bridesmaid's Basket

Designed for an older bridesmaid or matron of honour, this trug-shaped basket is spilling over with wild blooms to complement the bride's head-dress.

MATERIALS
rattan basket
snowberry
pittosporum
white and blue delphiniums
scabious
poppy heads
white veronica
cornflowers
nigella
lavender
cow parsley (Queen Anne's lace)
ribbon

EQUIPMENT
plastic lining
florists' foam (oasis)
silver and stub (floral) wire
scissors

1 Insert the plastic lining into the rattan basket, and place the soaked foam in the centre. To secure it, stretch a length of wire from one end of the handle to the other, pressing it into the foam. Pull the wire tightly, before twisting it around both handles.

2 Select the foliage and flowers to be used. These should coordinate with the bride's bouquet. Begin by building up a base of foliage using the snowberry and the pittosporum. Follow the shape of the basket, overlapping the edge by at least 5 cm (2 in).

3 The largest-headed flowers, delphiniums, are positioned first, then the next largest, and so on. The only flowers to be wired in the basket are lavender. These are grouped and fixed together to create a thicker, stronger stem, far easier to insert into the foam.

4 The last flower to be inserted is the cow parsley (Queen Anne's lace). This should fill out any gaps that may have appeared. Stagger the height of the flowerheads to give added depth.

5 Make a bow by taking a length of ribbon 20 cm (8 in) long and tie it once around the basket handle. Take another length of ribbon (approximately 1 m (40 in) long) and shape it into a figure-of-eight twice. Gather the binding point between your fingers, and tie it onto the handle ribbon.

WOODLAND WEDDING

moluccella

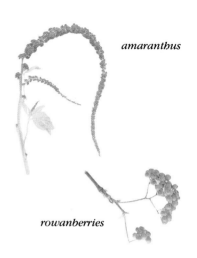

amaranthus

The idea of using greenery alone may at first seem a little strange, and perhaps unimaginative. However, once you take a closer look at the massive variety of foliage available, you will be amazed by the shapes, sizes and texture, not to mention the scope of colours, from the deepest green through to lime, bronze, red, silver and even black. The choices are endless, and a little imagination is all you need to create unforgettable arrangements.

viburnum berries

rowanberries

Bridesmaid's Head-dress

This very simple, full circlet uses a framework of birch twigs on which the ivy is loosely wrapped to give a natural effect. Onto this, bunches of rowanberries and alchemilla are wired at regular intervals; the vibrant orange and vivid green make an interesting contrast.

MATERIALS
birch twigs
ivy trails
rowanberries
alchemilla

EQUIPMENT
scissors
silver and stub (floral) wire

1 Create the circlet shape by twisting the birch twigs around each other, bending them into shape and binding them with wire at strategic weak points.

2 Loosely twist ivy trails around the framework and position the rowanberries and alchemilla as for the Bridesmaid's Hoop.

Bridesmaid's Hoop

This large-scale version of the bridesmaid's head-dress is simplicity itself, and completes the rustic feel of the ensemble. The natural materials used make it equally suitable for a younger bridesmaid or page boy.

MATERIALS
birch twigs
ivy trails
rowanberries
alchemilla

EQUIPMENT
scissors
silver and stub (floral) wire
gutta percha (floral) tape

2 Estimate the size of the final hoop, and tie the last loose twig ends together with wire to secure them.

1 As with the circlet, twist a few pieces of birch twig around one another, staggering and bending them into shape as you go. Bind any weak spots with wire.

rowanberries

3 Wrap the ivy trails loosely around the hoop to cover it almost completely and evenly. Do not be sparing. Ensure that all the wired points are hidden by the ivy.

4 Wire large groups of rowanberries together and tape them. Push these through the hoop at regular intervals.

5 Repeat as for step 4 using wired bunches of alchemilla.

Bride's Bouquet

The different groupings of unusual greens in this sheaf-style bouquet, makes a bride's spray of startling originality. It is the combination of colour and texture that makes the sheaf such a fascinating focal point: the soft brown velvet of the elegant bulrushes; the green furriness of the amaranthus; the bristles of the spiky red bottlebrush; the vibrant green fluffiness of the alchemilla; the smooth rounded lines of the grouped red viburnum berries; the crinkles of the two-toned sorrel, mixing delicate peach with deep bronze.

An added advantage of an arrangement like this is that it not only looks wonderful, it smells marvellous too. Fresh mint, marjoram and rosemary give off a heady herbal bouquet that is intoxicating.

MATERIALS
palm leaves
bulrushes
green amaranthus
rosemary
sorrel
viburnum berries
rowanberries
alchemilla
moluccella
wheat
bear grass

blue thistle
mint
red amaranthus
bottlebrush
marjoram
fatsia leaves
aspidistra leaves
ribbon

EQUIPMENT
scissors
string or garden twine

3 The viburnum berries, with their large clumps of red-yellow heads, are used here as the focal point. The roundness of the berry clumps creates a balance with the spiky and pointed foliage already used.

4 Keep adding the different types of foliage, angling them slightly and binding as you go, gradually building up the desired shape and profile.

1 Begin by taking the first two pieces of green, a palm leaf and a bulrush, to create a natural point which will determine the ultimate height of the sheaf-like bouquet. Decide on the binding point, which is usually about two-thirds down, and secure the garden twine around the stems.

2 Working in sections, start with one type of foliage in one corner, to create a grouped effect. Continue to build up the general shape, with green amaranthus, rosemary and sorrel, remembering to twist the garden twine around each stem to hold it in place, before adding the next.

5 Continue building the design, creating a contrast of colours and textures to evoke interest and surprise.

6 Frame the finished sheaf with strong-stemmed foliage, fatsia leaves and aspidistra. These protect and support the more delicate stems, and also accentuate the sheaf shape. Tie off the garden twine, trim the stems and tie with a bow.

Corsage

A contrasting cluster of orange and blue makes this sweet-smelling corsage the perfect finishing touch for mothers of the bride and groom. The unusual materials can, of course, be adapted to match the colours of individual outfits.

MATERIALS
rosehips
ivy leaves
marjoram
rowanberries
bottlebrush
sorrel
rosemary
moluccella

mint
blue thistle

EQUIPMENT
scissors
silver and stub (floral) wire
gutta percha (floral) tape
dressmakers' pin

1 Select and prepare the foliage to be used by wiring and mounting it on support wires where necessary (rosehips with heavy, bulbous heads, for example, need support). Tape each wired stem. The ivy leaves should be individually stitched and taped. Delicate stems, such as the marjoram, should be wired in bunches. The rowanberries should also be grouped for greater effect.

2 Choose the smallest heads first, or a pointed tip such as bottlebrush, and the smallest ivy leaves to begin the 'straight spray'. Gradually introduce the larger heads and leaves as you progress. Each new addition is taped to the previous one to secure it.

3 The binding point is positioned behind the focal group of heads, the rosehips. Trim any excess false legs as you go. This will ensure a slim, neat and light false stem. The spray is now at its widest and highest point. The binding tape should not change position from this point.

4 The remainder of the spray (the return end) is half the length of the top section. Build up the heads in the return end to meet the centre group of the spray, always keeping the binding point in the same position. To finish the stem of false legs, cut the excess false legs to about 2.5–4 cm (1–1½ in) below the binding point at the centre. Now, taper them to make a slender false stem. Cover the false stem with tape. Supply a pin to attach the finished piece.

Bridesmaid's Bouquet

For bridesmaids, this smaller adaptation of the bridal bouquet focuses on the same principal materials and uses the same method of assembly. Again, it takes the form of a small sheaf and should be held in the front-facing position, ideally by a younger bridesmaid.

MATERIALS
bulrushes
green amaranthus
rosemary
sorrel
viburnum berries
alchemilla
moluccella
bear grass
blue thistle

mint
bottlebrush
marjoram
fatsia leaves
aspidistra leaves
ribbon

EQUIPMENT
scissors
string or garden twine

1 As with the Bride's Bouquet, take the first two stems of foliage to determine both the height and shape. Bind them together tightly with twine.

2 Build up the sheaf shape by adding the groups of foliage at angles to create a fan-shaped effect. Although the spiralling method is used here, the added security of the twine will ensure that no piece of foliage will move out of place.

amaranthus

mint

3 The alchemilla is placed at the base of the posy to add lightness to the very compact arrangement and build the profile of the sheaf, giving it a gentle curve from the side.

4 Tie off the binding twine, and trim the stems to the required length. Cover the binding point with a suitable ribbon and bow.

Singapore orchid

ORIENTAL WEDDING

The allure and mystery of the East makes a stunning and innovative theme for a wedding display. Combining the best of Western floral design with Eastern-style blooms – Singapore orchids, cymbidium and willow – the bride's bouquet creates a spectacular waterfall effect which captures all the excitement of the Orient. This is echoed in the bride's head-dress which cascades from the back of the head to the nape of the neck. The flowers for the bride's attendants complete the theme.

cymbidium

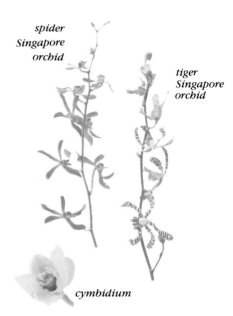

spider Singapore orchid

tiger Singapore orchid

cymbidium

Bridesmaid's Posy

This loose and light, hand-tied bouquet simply uses Singapore orchids and bear grass to provide an ideal foil to the luxurious abandon of the bride's bouquet. It is especially suitable for a younger bridesmaid.

MATERIALS
bear grass
long Singapore orchids
ribbon

EQUIPMENT
scissors
string or garden twine

1 Take a small bunch of bear grass for the centre of the bouquet and begin to build it up by crossing stems of Singapore orchid around this bunch.

2 After every five stems or so of orchid, add another small bunch of bear grass, spiralling as you go. Tie with string and cover with ribbon.

Bride's Head-dress

Worn at the back of the head in Oriental fashion, this attractive head-dress is arranged in the same way as a corsage, and is therefore simple to achieve. The weight of the piece is focused at the top, balanced by the cascading trails of green amaranthus.

MATERIALS
cymbidium heads
amaranthus leaves
ornamental cabbage leaves
Singapore orchid heads
palm leaves
green amaranthus trails

EQUIPMENT
scissors
silver and stub (floral) wire
gutta percha (floral) tape

2 Attach the second pink cymbidium head to the side of the first, in the same way. The third and final green cymbidium should be positioned to the side of the second, and taped in place.

1 Wire and tape all the material to be used. Place your first pink head of cymbidium over the first amaranthus leaf and bind them together with tape.

3 Frame one side of the head-dress with more amaranthus leaves and the other with ornamental cabbage leaves. Fill in the gaps between the heads with the smaller Singapore orchid heads.

4 Begin the return (lower) end by bending an amaranthus leaf back in the opposite direction to the first, and binding it together with tape. The binding point should be behind the third cymbidium head.

5 Insert small wired bunches of palm spikes at the bottom of the spray, with the trails of green amaranthus flowing downwards over the top of them. Cover the false handle with tape, then cut it to the required length.

Bride's Bouquet

This wildly romantic, tumbling waterfall effect is made possible by selecting materials with a natural kink or twist to them. By using the flowing qualities of the green amaranthus and Singapore orchid, a cascading framework provides a free, exuberant style – the perfect antidote to rigid, wired pieces.

amaranthus

MATERIALS
palm leaves
contorted (corkscrew) willow
green amaranthus
cymbidium
Singapore orchids
bear grass
ribbon

EQUIPMENT
scissors
string or garden twine

cymbidium

amaranthus

1 Take the two longest stems of palm leaves and cross them, one over the other. These will form the framework to the lower part of the bouquet. Insert a piece of contorted (corkscrew) willow at an angle, so that it bends downwards.

2 Now introduce the trailing amaranthus. Spiral the stems as you go. Build up the rest of the green base by adding a few more, shorter stems of palm leaves. One should be placed vertically to add length.

3 Weave the contorted willow evenly throughout the bouquet. Now introduce the cymbidium deep into the centre of the arrangement for depth and focus, with the longest stem trailing downwards to the floor.

4 Begin to add the long Singapore orchids evenly around the edge of the bouquet, with the shorter pieces towards the centre and top.

5 Finish it off by framing the hand-tied bunch with bear grass to soften the edges and give a wilder feel.

6 Tie the binding point with string, and cover it with a suitable ribbon.

Bridesmaid's Basket

This is a delightful little basket of different-coloured Singapore orchids, set off by a matching ribbon. Its small size makes it ideal for a young bridesmaid, although it is very simple to make on a larger scale.

cymbidium

MATERIALS
small rustic basket
palm leaves
Singapore orchids
ribbon

EQUIPMENT
plastic lining
florists' foam (oasis)
silver and stub (floral) wire
scissors

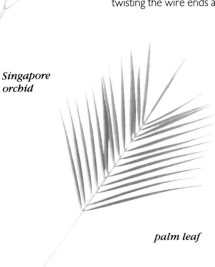

Singapore orchid

palm leaf

1 Insert the plastic lining into the basket and place the soaked foam in the centre. To secure it, stretch a length of wire from one end of the handle to the other. Press it slightly into the foam, twisting the wire ends around the handle.

2 Create the frame and base, with wired bunches of palm spikes positioned evenly over the foam.

3 Begin to introduce the orchids, one type at a time, again distributing them evenly over the foam, ensuring they protrude over the edge of the basket.

4 The white Singapore orchids have the largest heads, so use them for focus and depth. Position the buds around the outside of the arrangement.

5 Finish by tying a suitable bow at one end of the handle.

Bride's Bouquet

The hallmark of the Victorian posy is its neat circular bands of flowers, arranged regularly around a central bloom. But what sounds like a simple idea can take time, and patience to achieve; each flowerhead is wired individually. However, when properly done, a Victorian posy can look simply magnificent.

laurel

MATERIALS
dried lavender
dried red roses
glycerined eucalyptus
dried echinops
dried poppy heads
laurel leaves
ribbon

EQUIPMENT
scissors
silver and stub (floral) wire
gutta percha (floral) tape

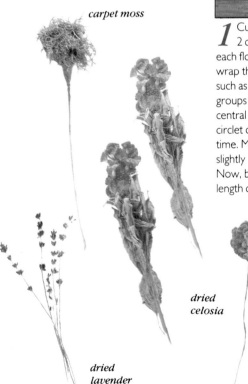

carpet moss

dried celosia

dried lavender

1 Cut all the stems down to about 2 cm (¾ in) and double leg mount each flower with stub (floral) wire and wrap them with tape. Delicate stems, such as the lavender, should be wired into groups and then taped. Holding the central rose in one hand, add the first circlet of heads, the eucalyptus, one at a time. Make sure that the central flower is slightly higher than the surrounding heads. Now, bind the circlet with a continuous length of silver wire.

2 For the next circle, use larger flowerheads, for example echinops, and position them slightly lower than the first. Carry on binding every stem into place with silver wire.

3 Continue to bind in the materials, to create a regular pattern. Use only one kind of flower for each circle, rotating the posy in your hand. The dome shape will start to form.

4 Carry on with this method until the required size has been reached. Finish off the arrangement with a circlet of green laurel leaves, to frame and support the flowerheads within.

5 Break off the wire, and trim the handle to the required length and width. Secure the handle with a suitable ribbon, wrapping it around the handle tightly, and finish with a bow.

Bridesmaid's Pomander

Popular in Victorian England, traditional, sweet-smelling pomanders make an interesting adornment for bridesmaids. This uncomplicated version is built around a dried ball of foam, using head-to-head roses interspersed with eucalyptus.

eucalyptus

dried roses

MATERIALS
red ribbon
dried red roses
glycerined eucalyptus

EQUIPMENT
scissors
silver and stub (floral) wire
dry foam ball
glue gun

1 Bend a long stub (floral) wire in half and push the wire ends into the foam until both ends protrude, and there is only a little metal loop left at the other end. Now bend the wire ends back and pull them back into the ball.

2 Attach a length of ribbon securely to the loop end. Remove all the rose heads from their natural stems.

3 Using a glue gun, place a drop of hot glue on the underside of the rose heads and stick the heads to the foam.

4 Begin by making a circle of roses all around the middle, working from top to bottom.

5 Now turn the pomander 90 degrees and stick another row of roses down the centre dividing the pomander into quarters.

6 Fill in the quarters with the remaining rose heads, and then begin to insert small pieces of eucalyptus between the rose heads to hide any holes.

7 Take the two ends of the ribbon and tie a knot to the required length. If a very small child is to carry the pomander, remember not to make the ribbon handle too long. Finish with a bow.

TRADITIONAL WEDDING

Casablanca lilies

F or many traditionalists, formal wired wedding designs are the only choice. Here they have been interpreted with a classic, elegant peaches-and-cream look.

long ruscus

Bridesmaid's Basket

The bridesmaid's basket gives a great opportunity to highlight the stars of the bride's bouquet, namely the Oceana roses and Casablanca lilies.

MATERIALS
rattan basket
long ruscus
sedum
Casablanca lilies
Oceana roses
ribbon

EQUIPMENT
plastic lining
florists' foam (oasis)
silver and stub (floral) wire
scissors

2 Insert the Casablanca lily heads, the buds on the outside and the more open heads in the centre.

1 Insert the plastic lining into the rattan basket and place a suitable-sized piece of soaked foam in the centre. Secure it with wire. Form the shape of the arrangement with the foliage, placing the ruscus in for definition, and filling in the holes with the sedum.

3 Place the rose heads around the lilies, until the arrangement is evenly covered. Finish with a bow.

Corsage

Lilies would not be appropriate in this corsage because of their size, but the piece complements the larger displays by using roses and the same foliage.

MATERIALS
rose leaves
ivy leaves
Oceana roses
eucalyptus

EQUIPMENT
scissors
silver and stub (floral) wire
gutta percha (floral) tape
dressmakers' pin

3 Introduce two more rose leaves vertically, at opposite ends, and place the focal rose between them, also vertically. Fill in any holes between the roses with clusters of eucalyptus.

4 Place the third and final rose at a diagonal to the focal rose, framing it with two ivy leaves at opposite ends, and a rose leaf to create the return end point. A pin should be supplied so that the finished piece can be attached.

1 Wire each piece of foliage and flower individually, and wrap it with tape. Now, take a stub (floral) wire and attach the first rose leaf to the end of it, and secure it into place with tape.

2 Add an ivy leaf on either side of the first rose leaf, then introduce the first rose.

ivy

Oceana rose

Bride's Bouquet

The danger with some wired shower bouquets is that the wiring can dominate the display, giving a stiff, formal feel to the whole arrangement. This problem has been overcome by wiring the blooms and greenery halfway down the natural stem, thereby allowing more life-like movement to the spray.

MATERIALS
long ruscus
ivy trails
eucalyptus
Oceana roses
Casablanca lilies
fatsia leaves
ribbon

EQUIPMENT
scissors
silver and stub (floral) wire
gutta percha (floral) tape
string or garden twine

3 Continue to introduce the roses on either side of the first one at appropriate intervals, as you did with the foliage, until the widest point of the bouquet has been reached. The most open roses are placed as near the binding point as possible. Begin to insert the Casablanca lilies. Again, the buds form the longest points and are slightly recessed for depth. The most open buds are positioned around the binding point to create a focus. About two-thirds of the overall bouquet length will now have been completed.

4 Begin the return end by binding a stem of ruscus to form the total length of the spray. Place the remaining foliage on both sides of the ruscus, beginning at the top and working towards the centre, forming the outline as you go. The fatsia leaves are placed at the back of the bouquet to provide support and definition to the main flowers.

1 Arrange the flowers roughly into the shape required by laying them on a table, making sure you have the right length of stems to form the cascade effect. You will need more than one stub (floral) wire with some of the longest flowerheads and foliage to achieve the correct length of stem. Cut all stems to the required length. Take the longest stem of ruscus and bend the false leg right back, to form the handle. The point at which the wire is bent is the binding point. Attach your silver wire to the binding point and begin to build up the shower shape of the bouquet.

2 Add shorter stems of foliage on either side of the longest piece of ruscus, graduating each piece carefully to retain the 'V' shape. Each stem is bound into position with the silver wire. Place a mirror in front of you to see exactly the shape you are building. Add your first and longest stem of rose on top of the first ruscus stem. This rose should also be the most tightly closed.

5 Finally, bind in the central material, making sure the central lily and rose are placed in vertically.

6 Cut and taper the stems to form an elegant handle. Twist the silver wire around the handle, working up and down to secure it, and then break it off. Now wrap the handle with a suitable ribbon, twisting it down the stem first, and then back up again. Fix a bow at the top of the handle, just by the binding point.

Bride's Head-dress

To complement an intricate shower spray such as this, we selected a simple, crescent-shaped head-dress for the bride. Echoing the theme of peaches and cream, it features seven perfectly shaped Oceana roses, carefully arranged with selected greenery. The understatement of this straightforward head-dress provides the ideal foil for the bride's bouquet.

MATERIALS
Oceana roses
ruscus
eucalpytus

EQUIPMENT
scissors
silver and stub (floral) wires
gutta percha (floral) tape

3 Add the three most open roses in a vertical line across the spray, to create both the widest point of the head-dress and the focus. Again, fill in the gaps with the clusters of foliage.

4 The return end should be a mirror image of the first. Always keep the binding point behind the focal rose. Place the last cluster of ruscus behind the last rose to balance the first side.

2 Stagger two roses on either side of the first and surround these with the clusters of foliage. Wrap each piece into position with tape.

1 Wire and tape seven roses, and several clusters of ruscus and eucalyptus leaves. Place the first rose on top of the first cluster of leaves and bind them together with tape.

ruscus

Bridesmaid's Head-dress

For the younger bridesmaid, the keynote is simplicity; anything complicated would compete unnecessarily with the magnificent bridal spray. A hairband makes an ideal choice, punctuated with Oceana roses in matching peach, and evenly spread with ivy.

MATERIALS
ivy leaves
Oceana roses

EQUIPMENT
scissors
silver and stub (floral) wire
gutta percha (floral) tape

1 Wire all the ivy leaves and roses separately and wrap them with tape. Make your mainstay wire by placing the ends of two stub (floral) wires together and binding them with tape. Make 6 loops 2.5 cm (1 in) long, from silver wire, bind with tape and bind to the mainstay wire at regular intervals. These will be used to secure the head-dress into place with hairpins. Take your first ivy leaf and attach it to the mainstay wire with tape. Place the first rose on top, and bind it in the same way.

2 Stagger the leaves and roses at regular intervals along the mainstay wire, cutting out any excess wires as you go to avoid undue thickening of the mainstay wire.

Oceana rose

3 Position the central rose vertically, so that it is facing directly forwards, to provide the focus.

4 Complete the second half of the head-dress in the same way as the first, saving the tightest rose for last, to give a slight taper.

DECEMBER WEDDING

gloxinia

gloriosa

gold-sprayed rose

viburnum berries

snowberry

*C*hristmas is a joyous choice for wedding festivities. The warm, seasonal colours of golds, reds and greens are reflected in all the flowers. Each flower brings its own special charm to the occasion; the gloriosa with its gold edging and the bell-shaped gloxinia. Add to that blue pine (spruce) and red berries, and the scene is set for a wedding that is warm and welcoming.

Bridesmaid's Basket

The basket is lined with blue pine (spruce) and filled with snowberry and gold and red blooms. Groups of red berries finish the arrangement.

MATERIALS
cone basket
blue pine (spruce)
snowberry
gold-sprayed cardoon
gold-sprayed red roses
gloriosa

viburnum berries
gold ribbon

EQUIPMENT
plastic lining
florists' foam (oasis)
silver and stub (floral) wire
scissors

1 Insert the plastic lining into the pine cone basket and place a piece of soaked foam in the centre, secured with wire. Now cover the foam evenly with sprigs of blue pine (spruce) and snowberry.

2 Begin to add the flowers starting with the largest heads. Work in staggered diagonal lines across the length of the basket. Insert the clusters of berries between the flowerheads. Attach a bow to one side of the handle.

Bride's Head-dress

This floral tiara of blood reds and warm golds is ideal for the Christmas bride. The roses are lightly sprayed with gold to create a two-toned effect. The berries form a natural taper at either end of the coronet, gradually building up into an explosion of colour at the centre. On a bed of gilded ivy, the individual heads are wired together to give a compact crown.

MATERIALS
gold-sprayed ivy leaves
viburnum berries
gold-sprayed red roses
gloxinia
gloriosa
gold-sprayed cardoon

EQUIPMENT
scissors
silver and stub (floral) wire
gutta percha (floral) tape

1 Cover a stub (floral) wire with tape. After removing the flowers from their original stems, mount each head, ivy leaf and cluster of berries onto silver wire using a double leg mount. Bind them with tape. Take the stub wire and attach the first gold ivy leaf and cluster of berries with tape, starting approximately 7.5 cm (3 in) down the wire and placing it to the left of the wire. Next, bind a grouping of four gold ivy leaves to the stub wire, alternating the sides as you go.

2 Introduce a group of three roses, slightly off-centre. Bind these in with tape. For the widest point of the crescent, add three gloxinia blooms, gathered closely together.

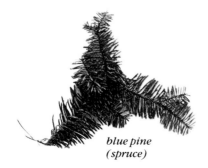

blue pine (spruce)

3 Frame the gloxinia heads with gold ivy leaves. Bind in three heads of gloriosa and two heads of gold cardoon, always working in groups. Begin to taper the crescent to form the return end of the head-dress.

4 From here on, the sequence of the flowerheads and foliage is a mirror image of the first side. Work through to the last gold ivy leaf, which should slightly overlap the end of the wire. Any excess wire should be trimmed and bent around to form a loop.

Bride's Bouquet

The deep reds and rich velvety textures of this luxurious hand-tied spray make it a winning choice for the season of goodwill. The bouquet is assembled using the loose, spiralled method, to give an impression of wild abandon and enhance the natural beauty of the seasonal flowers.

Foliage plays an important part in the arrangement. Snowberry, with its light feathery leaves and small white berries, frames the bouquet, providing an interesting contrast to the heavy, gold-sprayed cardoon and dark tones of the blooms. With shimmering golds, fiery scarlets and red-hot berries, this bouquet blazes with colour.

MATERIALS
snowberry
viburnum berries
gloxinia
gold-sprayed cardoon
gold-sprayed red roses
blue pine (spruce)
gold-sprayed bear grass
ivy trails

gloriosa
ribbon

EQUIPMENT
scissors
silver and stub (floral) wire
gutta percha (floral) tape
string or garden twine

1 Take a long, full stem of snowberry to form the point of the bouquet, and add shorter stems of viburnum berries along the outer edges to complete the triangular-shaped framework. Angle each stem as you insert it into place to form a spiral.

2 Build up the body of the spray by adding more foliage and berries towards the centre. Space each piece of material evenly throughout the bunch.

3 Mount the gloxinia heads onto stub (floral) wires to form false stems and cover them with tape. Do the same with the cardoon. These tend to be quite heavy, so use two wires if necessary. Begin to add the flowerheads, using up one variety of flower before introducing the next. Smaller heads, such as the lightly gilded roses, should be spaced out around the edges, while the larger heads such as the gloxinia and cardoon are concentrated towards the centre to give the arrangement depth.

4 Always take into account the natural bend of each flower and piece of foliage, and choose their position within the bouquet accordingly. Wire three heads of gloriosa together and mount them on a stub wire. Cover the false stems with tape. The large frilly heads of the gloriosa provide good coverage. Tie all the stems together at the binding point with string and cover with a ribbon.

pine cones

snowberry

gold-sprayed cardoon

Christmas Garland

It takes time and patience to put together a blue pine (spruce) garland like this one – but it is certainly worth the effort. Designed to be held by two bridesmaids (or a bridesmaid and page boy), it is full of natural movement and colour. All the materials are wired on as densely as possible, in clusters, to give the piece a feeling of unabashed opulence.

gloxinia

gloriosa

MATERIALS
blue pine (spruce)
pine cones (natural and gold-sprayed)
gloriosa
walnuts
gloxinia
viburnum berries

gold-sprayed cardoon
ribbon

EQUIPMENT
scissors
string or garden twine
silver and stub (floral) wire

1 Take a length of string and cut it to approximately 90 cm (36 in). Make a small loop at either end, to feed the ribbon through later. Attach the silver wire just below one of the loops. Prepare your sprigs of blue pine (spruce) – those with three prongs (shaped like a fork) are ideal for this purpose.

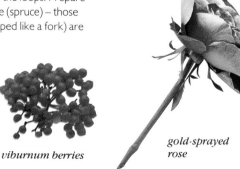

2 Attach the first sprig of blue pine onto the string by binding the silver wire twice around the base.

viburnum berries

gold-sprayed rose

3 Stagger the pieces of blue pine along the length of the twine, alternating the sides and rotating the body of the garland as you go. Each piece is individually bound in with the silver wire. Carry on using this method until you reach the end. Break off the wire.

4 Wire the pine cones by passing stub (floral) wire through and around the prongs of the lower part of the cone, twisting the two ends around one another. Now attach the cones in groups of three, placed at regular intervals along the garland.

5 Wire three gloriosa heads together. Arrange these triple heads in groups of three, by pushing the false legs through the body of the garland, bending them upwards, and back around the garland to secure them.

6 Continue to group clusters of flowers, berries and wired nuts at intervals along the garland until it is adequately covered. Pass the ribbon through the twine loops to make a larger loop at either end, and finish with a bow.

SPRING WEDDING

Springtime has been a time for great celebration since time immemorial. Bringing new hope and inspiration for the future, it is a fitting occasion for making vows, when new spring buds are bursting forth with their promise of a glorious summer. The designs for a springtime wedding feature egg-shaped tulips, feathery marguerites and anemones.

spray roses

variegated pittosporum

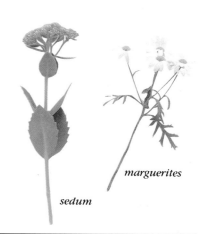

sedum

marguerites

Bride's Bouquet

The bride's bouquet is composed of various 'sections', grouped together to create an impression of abundance. The colours selected are yellows, whites and blues, the traditional colours of spring.

MATERIALS
variegated pittosporum
sedum
hebe
eucalyptus
yellow tulips
marguerites

purple anemones
white spray roses
ribbon

EQUIPMENT
scissors
string or garden twine

1 Prepare the materials by stripping the stems. Take the first two pieces of foliage and cross them to begin the spiral. Build up the foliage base until the desired shape is achieved – the foliage base should be quite dense.

2 Begin to add your first group of flowers, yellow tulips, concentrating on one quarter of the hand-tied bunch, until it is covered. Add the marguerites and anemones using the same method. Tie with string and a bow.

Bride's Head-dress

Like the bouquet, the head-dress is arranged in grouped sections. The focal point of the head-dress is the pretty speckled quails' eggs – a small novelty touch that complements the vivid colours of the springtime blooms.

MATERIALS
variegated ivy leaves
marguerites
purple anemones
yellow tulips
hebe
sedum
white spray roses
carpet moss

quails' eggs

EQUIPMENT
scissors
silver and stub (floral) wire
gutta percha (floral) tape
glue gun
glue sticks
long needle

1 Build a frame by overlapping two stub (floral) wires by 4 cm (1½ in). Bind them together with tape, working from the centre to the outside each time. Make a hook on one end and a loop on the other end. These should be 2 cm (¾ in) long, and bending outwards. Now prepare the leaves and flowers by wiring and wrapping the false legs with tape. The first ivy leaf should slightly overlap the end of the loop. All pieces are attached on the side of the frame with tape.

2 Begin to attach the flowers and foliage in groups, working from one side to the other, to form a pattern. Start with a cluster of marguerites, then move on to a group of anemones, and so on with the remaining materials.

quails' eggs

3 Continue to work around the frame until you reach the position where the quails' eggs are to be attached. Puncture both ends of each egg with the needle, and carefully blow out the yolk.

4 First, glue a clump of moss onto the frame, to cover the area where the quails' eggs are to be placed. Glue the eggs in place. Continue to work around the frame again, until you reach the hook. Join the hook onto the loop.

Bridesmaid's Basket

A pretty basket is an excellent choice for a bridesmaid.
This particular basket has been made to resemble a
nest, with the different elements grouped within it,
rather like a spring woodland scene.

anemone

ivy

MATERIALS
birch twigs
carpet moss
hebe
rosemary
sedum
pittosporum
yellow tulips
marguerites
white spray roses
anemones
quails' eggs

EQUIPMENT
chicken wire
silver and stub (floral) wire
glue gun
glue sticks
florists' foam (oasis)
scissors
long needle

1 Mould a piece of chicken wire into a bowl shape.

2 Make the handle by twisting a few birch twigs around one another, shaping them into an arch as you go.

3 Attach the two ends of the handle to opposite sides of the wire bowl with a strong stub (floral) wire.

4 Take a few pieces of carpet moss and pour glue evenly onto the underside of the moss with a glue gun. Press the sticky side firmly onto the inside of the wire bowl to create a nest effect.

5 Continue to glue moss onto the outside, shaping as you go.

6 Place a square piece of soaked foam into the centre of the nest. Secure it by stretching a length of wire from one end of the handle to the other, and pressing the wire a little way into the foam for added security.

7 As with the Bride's Bouquet and Head-dress, group sections of the nest beginning with the foliage, the hebe in one corner and the rosemary in the opposite corner.

8 Use up all the tulips to form a dense patch in one section of the nest. Now introduce a section of marguerites, followed by a corner of spray roses, and finally the anemones.

9 Blow the eggs as for the Bride's Head-dress, and glue three to five quails' eggs to the side of the nest, moulding out a little pouch for the eggs to rest in.

WEDDING STYLES

delphinium

phlox

*E*very wedding is unique, and how you choose to celebrate the occasion will be a reflection of your personality. The following pages illustrate just some of the many ways in which flowers can contribute to the style and theme you wish to express. All the plant materials used are clearly illustrated to use as a quick reference when deciding upon your floral designs. Draw inspiration from the many different arrangements to develop a style of your own.

veronica

eucalyptus buds

Sail Away

Nautical navy is a jaunty idea for a young page boy and bridesmaid in suitably Edwardian style – and being navy, it will blend in with almost any colour scheme for the bride's bouquet.

trachelium (throatwort)

PAGE BOY'S HAT
The Edwardian-style boater is decorated around the brim with white veronica and trachelium (throatwort). Seashells complete the nautical theme.

PAGE BOY'S BOAT
The boat is constructed from a base of chicken wire covered in moss, with white delphinium providing the sails. The sides are studded with eucalyptus buds to create portholes, and an anchor made out of wire and string finishes off the arrangement beautifully.

BRIDESMAID'S POSY
The bridesmaid's bouquet carries through the seashore imagery. The blue trachelium (throatwort) is interspersed with a selection of shells which are mounted on wire with glue. Shells and flowerheads decorate the bridesmaid's hair.

veronica

Thoroughly Modern Wedding

This contemporary design in classic white has clean, modern lines for the up-to-date bride.

BRIDE'S HEAD-DRESS

For the bride's head-dress, the key blooms are phalaenopsis orchid heads, tightly grouped with arum lilies for greater impact. Surrounded by clusters of ivy leaves and hebe, the crescent shape elegantly tapers to a point, with the dark, contrasting twigs of willow, used to equally dramatic effect in the bouquet.

BRIDE'S BOUQUET

Unlike conventional shower bouquets which demand heavy wiring, this contemporary version is cleverly structured using the natural curves of the flowers to give an impression of 'drop'. Swooping gracefully downwards in an elegant arc, the arrangement is carefully balanced by small selective groups of flowers whose natural lines merge at one central focal point; the Casablanca lily in the centre, framed by the three large-headed green arum lilies.

The edges of the loose, hand-tied shower are given the gentle touch with a halo of bear grass and long ruscus — an altogether softer and more sophisticated design for a modern wedding, with the accent on style.

As for colour, whites, creams and greens emphasize the clean, crisp lines and sheer simplicity of the modern minimalist theme. Less is definitely more.

arum lily

astilbe foliage

moluccella

hebe

Casablanca lily

pittosporum

fatsia

ruscus

Valentine Wedding

Tradition has it that the bride who weds on St Valentine's Day – 14 February – will enjoy the most blissful of marriages: after all, this is the one day of the year that is reserved solely for the celebration of love and lovers.

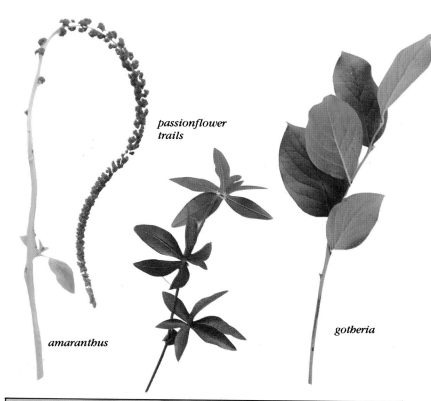

passionflower trails

amaranthus

gotheria

BRIDE'S HEAD-DRESS
The dramatic, tumbling effect achieved by this coronet provides a perfect frame to the bride's face. Drawing from a palette of deep, rich reds, the Nicole roses are perfectly counterbalanced by the viburnum and amaranthus.

GROOM'S BUTTONHOLE
Reflecting the four major elements of the bride's bouquet and head-dress, the groom's buttonhole focuses on the silvery-red Nicole rose. The single cascade of amaranthus gives this interesting grouping an extra dimension.

BRIDE'S BOUQUET

Appropriately, a dozen red roses – the traditional symbol of love – are at the heart of this Valentine wedding bouquet. What makes this bouquet unusual is the choice of rose. The Nicole rose is probably the most romantic of all flowers, a full, passionate, blood-red bloom, with a delicate silver tinge around the petals.

Brimming over with burgundy-red amaranthus and small clusters of viburnum berries, this cascading, loose, hand-tied arrangement makes a stunning display. The silver-toned green of the eucalyptus reflects the subtle underside of the Nicole rose perfectly, while the swooping bear grass gives a contemporary slant on romantic tradition.

Nicole rose

cinera eucalyptus

Pure and Simple

The classic white wedding arrangement is a perennial favourite. White Tineke roses combined with trachelium (throatwort) and only two varieties of foliage create a timeless display of understated elegance. The effect is simply stunning.

BRIDESMAID'S BASKET
White and wicker make a pretty combination for a delightful bridesmaid's basket, which is particularly suitable for a young girl. Selecting an unusual shape – in this case a rectangular basket – and packing it densely gives the arrangement a charm all of its own. Exactly the same flowers, trachelium and white Tineke roses, are used to complement the bride's bouquet, and the arrangement is given the finishing touch with a simple white silk bow.

cinera eucalyptus

Tineke rose

trachelium (throatwort)

BRIDE'S BOUQUET
For the ultimate in white weddings, the white bouquet is a fitting tribute. Its pure, clean lines command attention, and the choice of Tineke roses makes this a fairytale bouquet in true romantic tradition. Here, the traditional sheaf shape is designed to be carried by the bride in one arm, with the other hand supporting the hand-tied stems. Although white bouquets are very much a part of the traditional look, the ubiquitous gypsophila (so often playing a secondary role to roses in bridal bouquets) has been substituted with trachelium (throatwort), to bring a touch of the country to this timeless display.

Going Solo

The choice of a single-flower theme for a wedding is not as limiting as you might at first imagine. Take anemones, for example. With their great variety of colours, these exquisite blooms look glorious gathered up in a tight bunch. Nothing more in the way of foliage is required to enhance their delicate texture and deep hues.

anemones

BRIDE'S BOUQUET

A full, round hand-tied posy is packed with head-to-head anemones of all colours. The delicate, papery texture of the flowers makes this a most enchanting arrangement. Although carried here by the bride, this could also double up as a bridesmaid's posy. Anemones are at their most beautiful when used on their own without any additional foliage.

BRIDE'S HEAD-DRESS

This heavy garland head-dress is again tightly packed simply with anemones, to match the bridal posy. Each head is individually wired onto the base wire of the head-dress. Rich in depth and colour, this luxuriant crown with its full-blown blooms can be fitted directly onto the head and needs no attachments to keep it in place.

Pretty in Pastels

All the gentle shades of romantic summer pastels are combined in these country wedding flowers. The soft tones of pinks, creams and whites together with wispy strands of light grey eucalyptus draw attention to the large star-shaped heads of the stunning lily, the focal point of the arrangement.

*parvifolia
eucalyptus*

wax flower

Le Rêve lilies

BRIDE'S BOUQUET
The delightful informality of this bridal posy is achieved by the relaxed style in which it has been put together. Using the spiralled method, the stems are crossed at acute angles to ensure a wide circumference. The natural movement of the eucalyptus branches stabilize and protect the flowerheads, while at the same time allowing them freedom.

BRIDE'S HEAD-DRESS

The three large Le Rêve lilies grouped at the front give a natural peak to this tiara-shaped head-dress. Studded between lily heads and tapering at the sides are the delicate purple-tinged heads of eustoma. The darker clusters of wax flowers recessed into the head-dress provide depth and definition to the paler blooms around it. All flowerheads are individually wired and mounted onto a mainstay wire.

stock

cinera eucalyptus

eustoma

Everything is Coming Up Roses

For centuries the rose has been a symbol of true love, and there is nothing more romantic than the breathtaking profusion of rose blooms in this bouquet and coronet, invoking the exquisite beauty and heady fragrance of the rose garden.

No fewer than seven varieties of rose, combining bold colours and textures, delicate small heads and full-blown blooms, are gathered for the bridal flowers. The arrangement groups together colours – pale and dusky pink, softest white, soft yellow, blazing orange and the deepest red – all entwined with delicate trailing ivy. These extravagant bridal flowers beautifully complement the unconventional colour of the bride's dress.

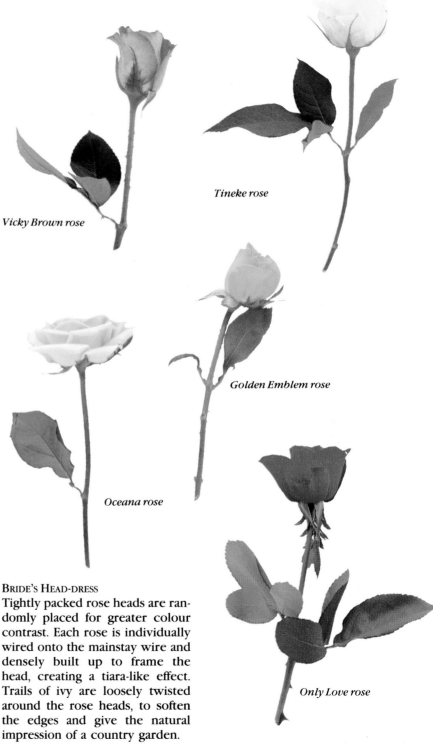

Vicky Brown rose

Tineke rose

Golden Emblem rose

Oceana rose

Only Love rose

BRIDE'S HEAD-DRESS
Tightly packed rose heads are randomly placed for greater colour contrast. Each rose is individually wired onto the mainstay wire and densely built up to frame the head, creating a tiara-like effect. Trails of ivy are loosely twisted around the rose heads, to soften the edges and give the natural impression of a country garden.

BRIDE'S BOUQUET

This large, hand-tied shower composed of seven varieties of rose is colour grouped to create the maximum effect. The overall impression is one of tumbling abundance, as if the blooms had just been gathered from the rose garden. While creating a very natural look with loose sprigs of ivy, twisting and trailing in all directions, an element of control is achieved by the blocks of colour and the size of the heads. The tighter heads are scattered around the edge of the spray, with the full-blown blooms concentrated towards the centre.

berried ivy

Jacaranda rose

Provençal Wedding

Sunflowers have always evoked long, hot summer days – the colours and sensations of the French countryside, with its azure skies, sweet-scented herbs and sun-scorched earth. Currently enjoying a renaissance in popularity, these eye-catching flowers look striking alone or combined with deep purple, standing out dramatically against the simple white muslin shift of the bride. For vivid colour and boldness, there is no equal to these stylish, self-proclaimed sun-worshippers.

gotheria

sunflower

hypericum

BRIDE'S BOUQUET
The perfect symmetry of the sunflowers is mirrored in the circular shape of this hand-tied posy. Six large heads make up the body of the bouquet, interspersed with splashes of purple agapanthus and the blood-red berries of the hypericum. This spiral posy is controlled within a framework of large, waxy gotheria leaves.

BRIDE'S HEAD-DRESS
Dominated by a cluster of sunflower heads, this crescent-shaped head-dress works best when worn slightly to one side. It is carefully balanced by dense patches of purple agapanthus and blood-red berries. A few twigs of contorted (corkscrew) willow sprout out of the far side of the head-dress: an irresistible indulgence.

Pastoral Wedding

Happy the bride who makes her vows in spring, the season made for new promises, with its connotations of re-birth and rejoicing. The simple combination of deep purple and pure white is used to full advantage to evoke a sense of cool freshness and elegant beauty. Tulips and anemones, in abundance at this time of year, epitomize springtime.

spray roses

ivy

anemone

smilax

BRIDE'S BOUQUET
This neat and simple hand-tied posy is composed of just two types of flowers: ivory-white tulips and deep-purple anemones. The well-defined lines of the bouquet make it an apt choice for a city bride or a quiet, intimate wedding. The regularity of the flowers coupled with the waterfall effect of the grasses add a stylish finishing touch.

tulip

BRIDE'S HEAD-DRESS
A garland head-dress made up of trails of smilax simply wound around a base wire is decorated with open tulip heads, white spray roses and deep-purple anemones. Each flower is individually wired and placed randomly around the circlet. The crown sits unaided on top of the head, pulled forward over the forehead.

Summer Wedding

Basking in bright sunshine beneath blue skies, a wedding celebrated at the height of summer will always be a day to remember. With full-headed blooms bursting forth, summer bouquets have a richness and opulence associated with no other season, and are resplendent in vivid, resonant colours.

aconitum

gotheria

ATTENDANTS' GARLAND
The long, flowing, and versatile garland looks impressive when carried between two young bridesmaids or page boys or, alternatively, it could be draped around a table or pedestal. Full and tightly arranged, it is deceptively light and well defined, thanks mainly to the small groups of aconitum bursting out between the hydrangea heads.

BRIDE'S BOUQUETS
This spiralled, hand-tied posy is a variation on a summer theme; the huge-headed hydrangea is a summer garden flower which produces magnificent blooms. For late summer weddings, the hydrangea makes an excellent alternative to the short-lived, early-summer peony.

eryngium

hydrangea

BRIDE'S HEAD-DRESS
A beautiful head-dress of pink peonies in full bloom provides a stunning accompaniment to the bride's bouquet. Densely packed with full flowerheads of purple aconitum and wax flower, it is also studded with clusters of miniature aconitum, picked from the lower stem of the main flower. The whole head-dress is finished off with trails of passionflower, wound between the peonies to soften the lines.

wax flower

peony

Harvest Wedding

As summer turns to fall, the woods and fields are ablaze with the colours of sunset. Leaves change to russet, burnt orange, gold and red, contrasting magnificently with the fertile evergreens. Like harvest time, an autumn wedding should be one of fruitful abundance, a celebration of living colour.

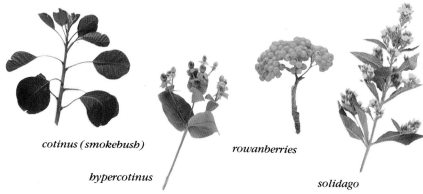

cotinus (smokebush)

hypercotinus

rowanberries

solidago

BRIDE'S HEAD-DRESS
This crescent-shaped head-dress, broadening across the forehead and narrowing at the side, provides a glorious complement to the bouquet. Berries and flower-heads are wired and tightly mounted in groups onto a stiff mainstay wire.

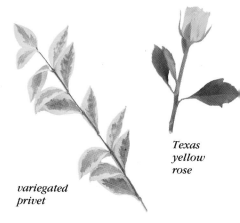

variegated privet

Texas yellow rose

BRIDE'S BOUQUET
The bride carries a spectacular hand-tied sheaf bouquet cradled in her arms, built up from an outline of ivy trails and long variegated foliage. The warm flame colours of the blooms are intermingled with rowanberries and sprigs of wheat. The stems are kept long to balance the weight of the front of the bouquet and, by using the spiralling method, the binding point is kept to a minimum allowing this bountiful bouquet to be held with ease.

Winter Wedding

Dazzling with its crisp, bright light and short daylight hours, the winter season imparts a natural incandescence to the bride it blesses. The beautiful Baccarola or black rose is an adventurous winter choice for the bridal bouquet. It takes its name from the dark, 'black' buds which open out to a velvety shade of blood red. In this arrangement, the blooms are illuminated fitfully by the golden light of the exquisite Singapore orchid.

Baccarola rose

BRIDE'S BOUQUET

This free-flowing hand-tied bunch takes full advantage of the natural bend in the Singapore orchid stem and the perfect roundness of the rose bloom. The bouquet is a lesson in simplicity; using just two types of flower, it creates a bold and memorable effect.

butterfly Singapore orchid

huckleberry

ivy trails

bear grass

BRIDE'S HEAD-DRESS

An unusual peacock-shaped head-dress designed to sit to one side of the wearer's head. The roses are grouped together at the base and the butterfly orchids burst forth from the floral crown.

Regency Wedding

The deep, vibrant colours and the silky, velvety textures of the various flowerheads imply all the richness of the Regency era. Bold and more than a little unconventional, the darker shades of pinks and purples make a brave choice for the bride who seeks a break from traditional pastels and whites. While working well with a white or ivory dress, this arrangement would look particularly spectacular with a truly adventurous choice of gown, in deep purple or green velvet.

variegated ivy

variegated pittosporum

cotinus (smokebush)

poppy head

BRIDE'S BOUQUET
This tight, hand-tied bouquet is created using the spiralling method to give an impression of fullness and roundness. Flower varieties are grouped in threes and twos to achieve an unusual effect; the bouquet looks different from every angle. The foliage has been specially selected for its colour, texture and shape to complement the richness of the blooms.

BRIDEGROOM'S BUTTONHOLE
Simplicity is style itself: a purple-pink arum lily with trachelium (throatwort) and poppy head surrounded by variegated ivy leaves, provide highlights from the hand-tied bride's bouquet.

Classic Circlets

What could be prettier than a combination of cream and pale yellow? Lemon-coloured roses and cream eustoma are punctuated by bunches of dark hypericum berries. The designs couldn't be more simple – matching circlets for the bride and her attendant, and a larger-scale floral hoop.

BRIDE'S HEAD-DRESS

The bride's head-dress has been constructed on a frame of thick stub (floral) wires taped together and bent around into a circle. Strands of smilax are then wound onto the circle frame. Smilax is particularly suited to this, as it is very light and bushy – an ideal, versatile material for the job. The head-dress is then decorated with lemon-coloured roses, cream eustoma and clusters of hypericum at regular intervals. The bridesmaid's head-dress is made in the same way, but slightly smaller.

eustoma

smilax

bouvardia

hypericum

BRIDESMAID'S HOOP

The bridesmaid's hoop makes a refreshing change from a basket or bouquet. Easy for little hands to hold on to, and particularly picturesque, it can still reflect the bridal theme by including the flowers used in the head-dress.

The hoop is made in the same way as the head-dress, on a larger scale. After the flowers have been inserted, paper ribbon is interwoven among the blooms.

Stars and Stripes

The novel Zebra rose is a newcomer to the flower scene, but already its distinctive colouring has marked it out as a bloom of true quality. Arranged in an attractive star-shaped posy, it is an unusual, up-to-the-minute departure for the modern bride.

Zebra rose

ruscus

gotheria

BRIDE'S HEAD-DRESS
Two concentric layers of ruscus and Zebra roses make up the body of this classic head-dress, designed to be worn around a simple chignon or hairpiece. Long ruscus stems are twisted around a stub (floral) wire until the wire is concealed. The roses are then individually wired, and placed at regular intervals around the ruscus and secured with stub wire.

BRIDE'S BOUQUET
Each perfectly shaped head is pressed against another to form a tightly massed bunch of cerise-and-white, striped Zebra roses. Edged with large gotheria leaves and sprigs of ruscus, this little posy is designed to be held at waist height, and accentuates the close-fitting line of the gown. Very light and manageable in size, the arrangement can double as a bridesmaid's posy.

Wedding Garlands

Should there be more than one bridesmaid, a garland makes an original alternative to a bouquet, and will look beautiful draped between them. Garlands flow naturally, and an abundance of blooms is ideal for a country wedding with a naturally rustic theme. The two garlands described here convey quite different images but both leave a lasting impression.

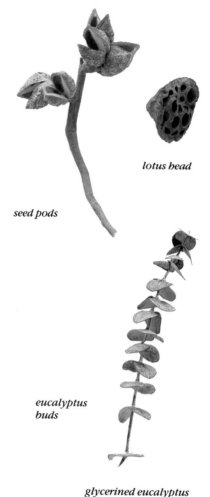

seed pods

lotus head

DRIED-FLOWER GARLAND

A framework of chicken wire covered with carpet moss provides the base for this elaborately adorned garland. The colours used are subtle in tone, but when grouped together they become more defined and striking. Each group of flowers is glued individually onto the base, at regular intervals, until it is completely covered. At each end, a large green taffeta loop and bow is attached with wire to form the handles.

dried mushroom

eucalyptus buds

glycerined eucalyptus

dried rose

FRESH-FLOWER GARLAND

Ivy trails are densely wound around a length of string until the required thickness has been achieved. Onto this are mounted clusters of sunflowers, wheat and berries at regular intervals – the sunshine and fruits of a long, hot summer in Provence. Finally, the rough, hay-like raffia is tied into a bow and looped at either end of the garland.

Colour Code

Colour matching different blooms is a novel way of creating a harmonious bouquet. In this case, the colour is pink, but not the safe, subtle pastel shades usually chosen for wedding arrangements – this is the bold, brash, ebullient colour of the full-blown amaryllis. To mix other colours here would certainly lessen the impact. The alchemilla is a fitting backdrop, pushing the flowers forward in all their glory.

alchemilla

amaryllis

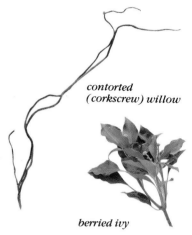

contorted (corkscrew) willow

berried ivy

BRIDE'S HEAD-DRESS

Designed in the same way as a corsage, this head-dress can be worn at the side of the head or at the back. It is composed simply of three large amaryllis heads grouped in a cluster, tapered at each end by a rosebud and softened by the sprigs of alchemilla. Willow is placed at the bottom edge of the head-dress, like a neat flash of inspiration.

rose

choisya

BRIDE'S BOUQUET

Roses and amaryllis have been grouped closely together to create depth of colour and texture in this circular hand-tied posy. Although the bouquet feels informal, the construction is carefully controlled. Each stem is spiralled in the hand with the alchemilla scattered through and around the bouquet to lighten the feel of the arrangement.

Scented Wedding

Using only one type of flower and one type of foliage, this type of arrangement is simple yet stunning, an ideal accompaniment to a dress in white or ivory.

BRIDESMAID'S HAND-TIED POSY
This fan-shaped, loose, hand-tied bunch of heavenly scented stock is beautifully offset by the bed of sage-green ruscus at the base. A large deep-purple silk bow is tied at the binding point for an elegant finishing touch.

stock

ruscus

BRIDE'S POSY
The bride's posy is a larger version of the bridesmaid's and assembled using the same simple method.

Dried-flower Designs

Dried roses can look every bit as stunning as their fresh counterparts – and the effects last for considerably longer. There is also something rather alluring about the colouring of dried flowers; they're altogether more subtle and gentle. Of course, part of this bouquet's beauty is that it can be prepared well in advance. And like all the best romances, this display will stand the rest of time.

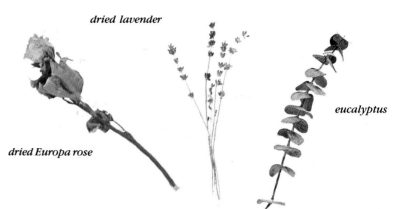

dried lavender

eucalyptus

dried Europa rose

BRIDESMAID'S BOUQUET
This tight hand-tied bouquet is packed with dried roses – there are some 80 heads in all forming a glorious dome shape, perfectly rounded. Interspersed with fragrant, dried lavender, the whole arrangement is finished with a large pale pink paper bow whose rough, ruched texture is reminiscent of the dried rose petals.

BRIDESMAID'S COMB
Designed to complement the dried bouquet, this elegant and discreet head-dress features an irresistible combination of yellow achillea and roses, blue delphinium, lavender and eucalyptus. It may be worn at the side or back of the head, depending upon the bride's hairstyle. Each flowerhead is glued onto the comb, and is much the same size and shape as a corsage, although there is no wiring involved in the construction of the arrangement.

Young at Heart

Flower arrangements for very young bridesmaids should take the child's size and age into account. These ideas are simplicity itself, using miniature blooms in pretty pastel shades.

Tiny spray roses make beautiful small spiralled posies or baskets for little hands to hold. The basket is constructed in a nest shape using chicken wire and carpet moss. The handle base is made from birch twigs covered with raffia and draped with passionflower trails for a natural finish. The little posy is simply spiralled and tied with a raffia bow.

sweetpeas

passionflower foliage

SWEET PASTELS
Simple to achieve and stunning to look at, pastel shades are as pretty as a picture, particularly for a younger bridesmaid. Anything more would detract from the freshness and charm of this bunch of sweetpeas, with its naturally scrunched effect. The added bonus with sweetpeas is that they smell as sweet as they look!

For the head-dress, sweetpeas in shades of pink, lilac and white have been arranged in their alternate colours around a bed of ivy leaves. Again, it is a simple yet effective idea which is quick and easy to achieve.

INDEX

ACKNOWLEDGEMENTS

The authors and publishers would like to thank the following for generously supplying materials for photography:

Gisella Graham Ltd
12 Colworth Grove
Browning Street
London SE17
(ribbons)

Pronuptia de Paris
20 Hanover Square
London W1
(bridesmaid's dresses)

Rebecca Street
294 Upper Street
London N1
(brides's dresses and wedding accessories)

Thanks are also due to the following for their invaluable help in creating this book:

Fleur Barber; Amy Barret; Edward Bennet; Hannah Bennet; Madeleine Brehaut; Daniele Bernstein; Nathalie Hammond; Antonia Jack; Hannah Jaffrey; Damien Kelleher; Emily Nurse; Susie Nurse; Philippa Perry; Rebecca Perry; Lindsay Porter; Adèle Rider; Amina Rookly.